THE
GREATEST SECRET
OF ALL

BY MARC ALLEN

Books

The Millionaire Course:
A Visionary Plan for Creating the Life of Your Dreams

The Type-Z Guide to Success:
A Lazy Person's Manifesto for Wealth and Fulfillment

Visionary Business:
An Entrepreneur's Guide to Success

A Visionary Life:
Conversations on Personal and Planetary Evolution

The Ten Percent Solution:
Simple Steps to Improving Our Lives and Our World

A Two-Second Love Affair (Poetry)

Spoken Word Audio

Stress Reduction and Creative Meditations (1 CD)

The Millionaire Course Seminar (3-CD set)

The Success with Ease In-Depth Course
(12-CD set with workbook)

Music

Awakening

Solo Flight

Quiet Moments

Breathe

Petals

THE
GREATEST SECRET
OF ALL

*Moving Beyond Abundance
to a Life of True Fulfillment*

MARC ALLEN

New World Library
Novato, California

New World Library
14 Pamaron Way
Novato, California 94949

Text design by Tona Pearce Myers

Library of Congress Cataloging-in-Publication Data
Allen, Mark, 1946–
The greatest secret of all : moving beyond abundance to a life
  of true fulfillment / Marc Allen.
    p.   cm.
ISBN 978-1-57731-619-0 (hardcover : alk. paper)
1. Self-actualization (Psychology) 2. New Thought.
3. Affirmations. I. Title.
BF637.S4A5733 2008
158.1—dc22   2007038651

First printing, January 2008
ISBN: 978-1-57731-619-0
Printed in Canada on 100% postconsumer-waste recycled paper

New World Library is a proud member of the Green Press
Initiative.

10   9   8   7   6   5   4   3   2

This book is dedicated
to you.

CONTENTS

THE
GREATEST SECRET
OF ALL

INTRODUCTION

*How I first discovered
the secret of manifestation,
and then the greatest secret of all*

Somewhere along the many paths I've taken, it became obvious to me that every one of us is completely unique. Every one of us is an original, even a creative genius, in some way or ways. We all have a long and winding and absolutely original path, and each of us makes our discoveries in our own way.

It can be helpful at times to hear another person's story; what has worked for me just might work for you as well. Feel free to skim through this Introduction, if you wish. Find the words that grab your interest, and skip the rest.

The core of this book is in Part One, Part Two, and the Summary. There, slow down and take in the words, especially in the Summary, which is just a few pages. You'll notice that I return to the key points again and again, stating them in different ways. The repetition is important, in my opinion; it can take a long time for us to absorb this kind of life-altering information, and each time we hear it or read it, it sinks in a little deeper.

Throughout the book,
the essential points are in bold, centered.
If you wish to quickly grasp
the essence of this book,
just read the key points.

I'll start with a bit of my story. Throughout my twenties and early thirties, I had the opposite of the Midas touch. Everything I touched fell apart. Worse yet, I was on an intense emotional roller coaster much of the time, with a variety of anxieties and periods of immobilizing depression.

I dropped out of college to join a theater company that fell apart within a year. I joined another company, and that fell apart too after just a few months. I wandered to a Zen center and got kicked out for breaking the rules. I tried a back-to-the-land experiment that only lasted a few cold, wet months. I spent over three years at a Tibetan Buddhist center, working very hard, making no money at all, and not making much progress in my understanding of anything that helped improve my unsatisfactory life.

I wandered around the spiritual smorgasbord of Berkeley, California, for a few years, living on almost nothing. I was fired as a busboy and dishwasher for being too slow. I was fired as a typesetter for not showing up on time. I had a rock band that lasted a few years before it broke up.

THE DISCOVERY

And then I turned *thirty.* I woke up in a state of shock, finally realizing I wasn't a kid anymore. I had no job and no savings or any other assets except an old torn-up electric piano. I was scrounging (a word we used often) to come up with $65 every month for rent for my little studio apartment in a funky part of Oakland, California.

That day changed my life, because I began to apply some ideas in some new ways, ideas that before had just been occasional floating thoughts, ephemeral and remote possibilities in my mind. I sat down and wrote on paper what became — for me, in my words — the first secret of manifestation:

The first step to discovering
the secret of manifestation
is to write your ideal scene on paper,
your dream life five years in the future.
Begin with the end in mind,
and keep it in mind.

The day I turned thirty, I sat down and took a sheet of paper and wrote *Ideal Scene* at the top. I imagined everything had gone as well as I could possibly imagine, and somehow, over the next five years, I was able to create the ideal life for me. What would it look like? What would I do and have, and who would I be?

I was surprised, even shocked in a strange way, at what came spilling out on paper. I imagined I had a publishing company, successfully publishing books and music, including my own books and music. Before I sat down and wrote out my ideal scene, I had absolutely no interest in business. I had never taken a business course. I had never written a book or recorded my music. The words that spilled out when I wrote my ideal scene surprised me as much as they were to surprise just about everyone else I knew.

I imagined I wrote successful books and recorded beautiful music as well. I imagined I had a lovely white home on a hill in northern California, one of my favorite places on earth. I imagined I had a wonderfully loving relationship. I dared to imagine my *ideal*, so I imagined I had plenty of time for it all: creativity, a successful business, friends and family, and plenty of free time alone for myself as well.

And I added something else that changed my life dramatically: When I dared to think of my *ideal*, the kind of life I would have if I could have anything at all, I realized what I really wanted was a life of ease. I didn't want to work too hard. The few forty-hour-a-week jobs I had tried hadn't worked out, and working that many hours felt inhumane to me. Ideally, I wanted plenty of time for ease and relaxation, plenty of time for my creative life, spiritual life, and personal life with friends and family.

That was my ideal: success with ease, and success without compromising the other things that were important to me in life. I wanted to do what I loved, and not have to do anything I didn't really enjoy.

I didn't know it at the time, but I was beginning to learn secrets that were far greater than the secret of manifestation.

*The simple step of
writing down my ideal scene
led me to discover the unfailing
natural laws of manifestation.*

I stared at that sheet of paper awhile and realized that within it was a list of goals. I took a second sheet of paper and listed all the goals I could think of. There were twelve of them, at first. (Now I'm down to six.)

It was thirty years ago, but I remember it clearly: As I was writing my goals, I was assaulted with doubts and fears. I wrote, "Start and build a successful company," and my thoughts were churning — *You? Who are you trying to kid? You have no money, and you need money to make money! You know nothing of business! You don't even like business! And it'll wreck your creativity! It'll destroy your soul! Money is the root of all evil! The rich man has as much chance of entering the Kingdom as a camel does of going through the eye of a needle!* On and on it went — an endless stream of doubts, fears, and darkly negative thoughts.

But then I remembered something I had read in a book by Catherine Ponder, a Unity Church minister. She wrote about the power of *affirmations* — simple statements or declarations that your dream or goal is now coming into being. They work best when they're in the present tense, worded in a way that your subconscious mind can accept and begin to absorb and play with.

The most vivid phrase I remember from Catherine Ponder's writing has become part of my daily life. She said that affirmations are even more effective if they start or end with this phrase: *In an easy and relaxed manner, in a healthy and positive way…*

So I took another sheet of paper and rewrote each goal as an affirmation, beginning with that phrase. I worded my goal of starting and building a successful business like this: *In an easy and relaxed manner, in a healthy and positive way, I am now building a successful business.*

> *The second step to discovering*
> *the secret of manifestation*
> *is to write your goals as affirmations,*
> *beginning with*
> **In an easy and relaxed manner,**
> **in a healthy and positive way…**

Years later, looking back, I realized how powerful those words were — so powerful, in fact, that by repeating them daily, I overcame many of my doubts and fears. What, after all, are our doubts and fears whispering to us? *It isn't easy; it's very difficult! It certainly isn't relaxed; it's stressful! It's not healthy for you, not even positive. You'll fail! You don't know what you're doing! You're a fool!*

That powerful little phrase — *in an easy and relaxed manner, in a healthy and positive way* — repeated thousands of times, overcame a lot of those doubts and fears. It took me about five years, but I finally got it through my thick skull that it was possible to create a great deal of success in the world in an easy and relaxed manner, in a healthy and positive way.

Don't underestimate the power of those words — or the power of any words you repeat to yourself. Our thoughts determine our actions. And our actions lead, inevitably, to success or failure, fulfillment or frustration.

I typed up my list of goals as affirmations and carried it around with me in my back pocket. I often began the day by reading that list. I read it at my desk as I started to work. I read it in the bathroom sometimes.

Some deep part of me knew that if I kept reading and rereading that list, my subconscious mind would absorb it sooner or later, and I would eventually be able to turn those distant, ephemeral dreams into solid intentions — and once that happened, those intentions would soon become reality.

Reading my list of affirmations led me to the next obvious step:

> *The next step to discovering the secret of manifestation*
> *is to write a one-page plan*
> *for every major goal.*

It's simple, isn't it? For me, the process has to be simple, and the words I write have to be words a child about ten years old can easily understand. That makes it much easier for my subconscious mind to absorb those words.

I took a separate sheet of paper for every major goal on my list and wrote a one-page plan to achieve that goal. This little process took several months for some of the plans, because I didn't even know where to start.

The only plan I could think of at first for starting a business involved just a few action steps: Read a used business textbook, and talk to anyone I could who knew more about business than I did. These little steps led me to see and then take the next step of actually writing a simple, one-page plan.

That led to the final step:

> *The final step to discovering*
> *the secret of manifestation*
> *is to take action.*
> *When you have a plan,*
> *an intention will form.*
> *When you take action,*
> *nothing can stop you.*

This step became obvious as soon as I'd taken the other steps. I kept reviewing my plans — and rewriting them, because most of them changed all the time — and then I'd pull out my little weekly calendar and write down an action step to take on a specific day. Without being consciously aware of it at first, I was sending a powerful message to my subconscious mind: Not only am I planning, in writing, to achieve this goal, but I am taking the next steps necessary to get there.

At age thirty I was a poverty case; about six years later I was a millionaire. The secret to success that had eluded me for so many years became simple and obvious to me:

Great success is the result
of a great many small steps,
all moving toward a clearly defined goal.
That is the secret of manifestation.

Maybe some of you are thinking it can't be that simple. Or you've heard it all before, and there's nothing new in it. It's true — there is nothing new in it, and you've probably heard it all before. And it *is* simple — these simple steps set your course. Then it's just a matter of ongoing course correction, of getting back on course every time you wander off course into doubts and fears, frustration and anxiety.

How do you get back on course? By focusing, once again, on your goals and affirmations, and remembering your plans and moving ahead on those plans in whatever way you can.

I once heard that an airplane is off course over ninety percent of the time. But the pilot just keeps correcting the course, over and over, and the plane finally reaches its destination. When I heard that, I thought, *That's the story of my life. I set my course, and then kept going off course, over and over. So I had to reset my course, over and over.*

That sums up the whole process for me.

THE VALUE OF EVERY MOMENT OF THE PAST

Once I set my course, I noticed a fascinating process begin to unfold. Before I went through those few simple steps on my thirtieth birthday, I had the image that all my past experience had come to nothing, that it had slipped away like sand through my fingers. But once I set my course, once I wrote a simple plan, I began to realize that every experience I'd ever had was valuable, and I had learned a great deal in my various activities and wanderings through my teens and twenties.

I had learned a great many valuable secrets, but I hadn't yet applied them in my life. The little steps I took the day I turned thirty changed all that. As soon as I affirmed my goals, made a short plan to reach those goals, and took the first few obvious steps in front of me, those simple actions somehow made me far more aware of so many things I had learned in the past. Instead of feeling as if everything I had learned had slipped through my fingers like sand, leaving me with nothing, I realized I had absorbed a great deal of information and knowledge that could help me reach my goals.

In my early twenties I worked about six months for one of the world's worst bosses — a miserable man who had learned the secret of manifestation but had no clue to the far greater secrets of a life well lived. I realized if I did exactly the opposite of what he did, I could become a good employer and leader. He taught me what not to do, and that's been invaluable to me all my life.

Another time in my early twenties I wandered into a bookshop in Madison, Wisconsin, that specialized in Western magic. I talked for maybe an hour with the owner and left with several books. That was my introduction to the Western mystical traditions, drawn primarily from the Kaballah, an esoteric branch of Judaism, and from Egyptian traditions.

The most memorable book I got at that time is one I still read to this day, *The Art of True Healing* by Israel Regardie. It is Western magic in a nutshell, and it gave me some exercises I still do fairly regularly, not only for healing myself and others, but for the creation of wealth and fulfillment as well. (The main reason I continue to do these exercises is that I do them flat on my back, in bed — the favorite kind of exercise for someone as lazy as I am.)

I began yoga classes when I was with my first theater company. It was tremendously healing for body, mind, and spirit, and I feel I'm still reaping the benefits of that yoga, though I'm too lazy to do much of it on a regular basis.

I began meditating at that time as well, and saw a vast new inner space open up, a world of the mind, created in an instant by the mind, and somehow connected to an inner source of creativity, abundance, and fulfillment. I discovered a quiet center within, from which we can create a far better life experience for ourselves and help others as well. I wasn't sure how to use these new tools that were given to me, but I began to see all kinds of new possibilities.

I went back to the Bible in my late twenties and reread the words of Christ. I collected the sayings of Christ — every word he said in the New Testament — in a little booklet and carried it around with me for a while. In very simple words, words a child can understand, Christ gave us both the secret of manifestation and the greatest secret of all.

Ask and you shall receive;
seek and you will find.
That is the secret of manifestation.

Love one another, as I have loved you.
Love your neighbors as yourself;
love your enemies.
That is the greatest secret of all.

How much simpler and clearer could these words possibly be? What authority and power are in the words of Christ!

The words of Catherine Ponder as well have stayed with me and affected every step I have taken. Actually, it was just that *one phrase* from Catherine Ponder that changed my life — a phrase you'll hear me repeat, over and over: *In an easy and relaxed manner, in a healthy and positive way...*

I studied Buddhism over the years, too, and found it is totally compatible with Christianity — and Judaism, and Islam, and every other religion that has a great vision at its center. Buddhism is more a practical philosophy and effective therapy than it is a religion, in the usual sense of the word. In Buddhism, there is nothing to believe, no Apostles' Creed. Buddha's last words to his followers were to accept nothing he had said as the truth until they tested it in their own experience and found it to be true.

Gradually, reading the words of Jesus, studying Buddhism, and meditating had their quiet influence on me, physically, mentally, and emotionally. Most of my anxieties were relieved over time, with very little effort, and my depression completely dissolved.

I began to understand that my anxieties didn't have an external cause; I was creating them myself through my own rampant thoughts and heedless activities. Over time, I realized that the world out there isn't doing it to me — I'm doing it to myself. We cause our own suffering.

Yes, we will certainly have physical pain at some times in our lives; just because we have physical bodies, pain is unavoidable — but suffering is optional. We are the creators of our problems — not anyone else, and not the vast world outside.

When Buddha touched the earth at the moment of his enlightenment, all his problems evaporated, never to return, for he understood that the cause of his problems was within his mind, and he was able, through this insight, to avoid causing any more problems for himself. His life changed in that moment: His suffering and frustration were completely transmuted into love, compassion, abiding serenity, and light.

When Buddha touched the earth, he discovered the greatest secret of all.

I had gathered a lot of very good information in my twenties, but it hadn't yet affected my life. The teachings of Christ, Buddha, meditation, yoga, and Western magic had been fascinating to me, but I was still a frustrated poverty case. The information had not become knowledge that affected my day-to-day experience; the knowledge had not become wisdom that guided my life.

As soon as I dared to dream the most expansive dreams I could, as soon as I dared to make a plan, in writing, to reach my goals, the information I had gathered over the years suddenly became something I could use: The information became knowledge that guided me, step by step, to discover the secret of manifestation and, more important, the greatest secret of all.

DEALING WITH DOUBTS AND FEARS

As soon as I dared to imagine my ideal scene, I was overwhelmed with doubts and fears. It is obviously essential to learn how to deal with all the inner voices that would sabotage us. That becomes the most important work of all, for if we let doubts and fears undermine our dreams, we will never be able to attain those dreams.

Our doubts and fears are our worst enemies, and our best teachers as well.

When I look back on it, there were just a few simple things I did to overcome most of my doubts and fears. The first one I've already mentioned: I started affirming that my goals were coming into being in an easy and relaxed manner, in a healthy and positive way. Those words alone became powerful creative forces for good in my life.

Another thing I did was to just make a simple decision. I remember my thirtieth birthday vividly, pacing up and down in my little slum apartment, talking to myself. My cat looked at me like he thought I'd gone crazy. I stopped pacing long enough to write down my ideal scene, and before I got the first sentence out I was inundated with doubts and fears.

They were all very sensible, realistic, and rational. *How can you possibly dare to dream of even a little success, much less a great success? Look at you, you're thirty years old and barely scrounging your cheap rent together every month. You're a fool with money. You're a poverty case. What makes you think you can change all that? You obviously don't have what it takes. Take a look around you and you know that's true!*

Those inner voices went on and on. But then I remembered something I'd heard years before. There was an inventor and visionary named R. Buckminster Fuller who did a lot of speaking, mostly at universities, in the sixties.

Someone told me he said that in his twenties he had come to a point where he decided to either commit suicide or look at his life as some kind of unique experiment. Fortunately for all of us, he chose the latter, and at the end of his life he said it had all been "a fifty-year experiment."

I latched on to that word *experiment*. I literally said out loud to all my doubts and fears, *Why not look at it as an experiment? Why not go for my dreams, purely as an experiment?*

My doubts and fears were quick to reply, *It can't possibly work. No way! Who are you trying to fool?* But I was able to say, *Look, if it doesn't work, I won't be any worse off than I am right now!*

My doubts and fears couldn't argue with that, though they were certain my experiment was a ridiculous waste of time. But I got around those doubts and fears by saying to them, *Give me a year or two to try this, purely as an experiment. If after that time I find out you're right, I'll have to agree with you and be more sensible and realistic. But I'm going to try this experiment, just because it seems like a good thing to do.* (And also because it allowed me to continue to be as lazy as I really wanted to be!)

The vast majority of my thoughts at the time were convinced I would fail. *How can you be as lazy as you want to be and still succeed in life? Impossible! It's never been done in the history of humanity!* But I was able to talk myself into taking my first tentative steps, *purely as an experiment.*

Within a year, I knew it would work. My life was still a struggle, but I could see enough signs to convince me that I was on the right track and that it was possible for me to create the life of my dreams in an easy and relaxed manner, in a healthy and positive way.

Another thing I did that overcame a great number of doubts and fears was to go through a process I had stumbled into during a weekend seminar in my late twenties. It was led by a man named Ken Keyes, Jr., the author of a book called *Handbook to Higher Consciousness.* During the weekend, we went through an exercise called the Core Belief Process. It involves asking yourself and answering a series of simple questions. I go through it in detail later, in Part One, so now I'll just give an example of it.

By my mid-thirties, I had started my own company and written some books and recorded some music, but it was still a chaotic struggle, financially and emotionally. Then I hit my financial low: The distribution company we had set up collapsed, we didn't get paid for six months of sales, and I had $65,000 of credit card debt, without the means to make even the minimum payments every month.

The company kept afloat — barely, miraculously — because we had just enough checks coming in from customers who bought directly from us, and I kept afloat only because banks kept offering me more credit cards. As soon as I got a new one, I'd run to the bank, get some cash out with the new card, and pay off my old minimum payments. I remember vividly the last time I had to do that. I was in my car on the freeway, heading to the bank, and I was agitated and frustrated. I remembered the Core Belief Process and said to myself, *This is the best time to do it — when you're upset about something.*

So I went through a list of simple questions, asking and answering them out loud while I drove down the freeway, alone in my car. This was before cell phones, and I caught several people looking at me as if they thought I had lost my mind.

I asked, "What is the problem?" The answer was immediate and forceful: *The problem is I'm nearly bankrupt. I'm in way over my head. Someday the bottom will fall out.*

"What emotions are you feeling?" *Frustration. Anger. Fear. Guilt. Sadness.*

"What physical sensations are you feeling?" *My neck is rigid, shoulders too — I'm uptight! My stomach is uncomfortable, anxious.* I was probably headed for an ulcer if this continued much longer.

"What are you thinking about?" *I'm a fool with money! I don't understand it. I can't save it. A fool and his money are soon parted. That's the story of my life, for sure. It's completely out of control. I can't manage it.*

"What is the worst thing that could happen in this situation?" *I could go bankrupt. My company could fail miserably.*

"What's the very worst thing that could happen?" *I could die, slowly and painfully, a drunken bum in the gutter, and no one would care or even notice.*

"What is the *best* thing that could happen? What would you like to have happen *ideally*?" For some reason, this was harder to put into words than even my worst fears had been. I had to think about it awhile, and then I said, *I know I'm not capable of budgeting my way out of this mess. Some people can do that, but not me. The best thing would be to have an explosive growth in our sales, and a great new distributor that pays us on time. Then we'd be solidly profitable and I'd have cash bonuses big enough to pay off all my credit cards and build my savings to the point where I could live off my savings and wouldn't have to work for a living.*

"What fear or limiting belief is keeping you

from creating what you want?" *I am a fool with money. I am out of control. I don't have what it takes. It's so hard to succeed.*

"What affirmation can you come up with that counteracts that negative or limiting belief?" The words that sprang to mind were startling: *I am sensible and in control of my finances. I am creating total financial success, in an easy and relaxed manner, in a healthy and positive way.*

Those words felt really good to me, and I pulled over on the shoulder of the road and wrote them down so I wouldn't forget a word. Later I wrote the affirmation down several times and put it in my pocket, on my desk at work, on the dresser in my bedroom, on the mirror in the bathroom. I kept it in front of my face and kept repeating it, especially when I'd start feeling all those old fears and anxieties again.

Within a matter of months, my financial situation improved substantially. We found a great new distributor. Our sales picked up. A new bookkeeper came along who definitely helped me become far more sensible and in control of my finances. (I am eternally grateful to Publishers Group West, for their excellence in distribution, and to Victoria Clarke, our CFO to this day, for her financial savvy and guidance.)

It finally dawned on me that managing money is simple, so simple that even someone like me can do it. You just need to find a way to make more than you spend — this was a new and foreign concept to me at the time — and then keep doing it consistently, so that over time you build wealth. You simply need to watch your spending so you reach the place where your income is greater than your expenses. This is not rocket science or brain surgery. This is something anyone can understand. Even me, a fool with money. Now that I understand it, I'm no longer a fool with money. Now I'm a magician with money — my savings and other assets earn more than I need, and I don't need to even lift a finger. That's magic, in my opinion — real, practical magic.

There was one other thing that happened at about that time — in my mid-thirties — that helped to quickly turn a disaster into a success. It involved just a single phrase I heard on the radio. Someone quoted Napoleon Hill from his book *Think and Grow Rich*: *"Within every adversity is the seed of an equal or greater benefit."*

I wrote that down and put it in big letters right by my phone on my desk, where I would see it almost every day. Later on I added to it: *Within every problem is an opportunity.* And years later I added a third phrase that I read in the prose version of the Bhagavad Gita that we published: *"Even in the knocks of life we can find great gifts."*

Those phrases turned my thinking around, many times, over many years. As I encountered the problems and obstacles that inevitably arose, I would ask myself, *What benefits could there possibly be in this situation? What opportunities? What gifts?*

And I found something wonderful and amazing (and those words are not exaggerations): When you ask that question, you get answers. And they're the perfect answers for you, because they come from within you, and they connect you to a powerfully creative source within.

What benefits can possibly come from being on the verge of bankruptcy? What opportunities? What gifts? As soon as I asked that, I realized I was in this mess because I hadn't taken full responsibility for the success or failure of my company. I kept looking for someone with more experience, more knowledge, to come along and rescue me and show me what to do. That person hadn't come along, so *I* had to be that person. The buck had to stop with me.

As soon as I made the decision to take the reins of my company — in spite of all my shortcomings and lack of experience and doubts and fears — I took control of the realization of my dreams in some new way. And I discovered that, as soon as I really took responsibility for the success of my struggling company, I found new strengths and knowledge I didn't know I had. Not only that, but other people came along as well and helped me immeasurably. They came along because I could show them the benefits and opportunities and gifts for all of us if we worked together to create a successful company.

A great benefit and gift from our near bankruptcy was that a team came together that knew how to build successful partnerships. We began to create win-win partnerships with everyone, and that soon led us to the point where I had completely realized the life I had dared to imagine when I asked the question, *What is the best thing that could happen?*

The dream of my ideal scene had seemed so insubstantial at first, and had brought up so many doubts and fears — and yet I managed to create the life of my dreams, in spite of all my doubts and fears, weaknesses and shortcomings.

I set my course clearly, and looked at it all as an experiment.

I affirmed I was creating total financial success, in an easy and relaxed manner, in a healthy and positive way.

I began to ask myself what the opportunities, benefits, and gifts were in every situation I was confronted with.

Slowly, over a period of several years, my doubts and fears became weaker and weaker. Those old paths through the synapses of my brain got fainter and fainter as I took new paths more often, based on new and far more powerful beliefs.

Slowly, my old beliefs changed — and, step by step, my dreams began to manifest, in an easy and relaxed manner, in a healthy and positive way.

THE GREATEST SECRET OF ALL

We have all had intimations and glimpses of the greatest secret throughout our lives. We have all heard the greatest secret many times.

When we discover it, it transforms our lives. We find it when we fall in love. We know it when we gaze into the eyes of our children. We know it whenever we become filled with joy and appreciation for someone or something. But then we forget it, over and over, and fall back into those old habitual fears and frustrations.

All we need to do is to remember this great secret again — and again, and again, and again. It has been said in so many different ways, in so many different words. Here's my attempt, in my words, to express it. These words feel a little stodgy to me; I put it in other words later that might speak more directly to you:

We have a great purpose in life —
a mission, vocation, and calling.
We are here to grow, to evolve,
to reach our full potential
and contribute to the betterment
of the world.

This is what has remained a secret for most of humanity: *We are far greater than we think we are.* Our potential is vast. Most of us have just barely begun to realize who we are and what we are capable of. We have had just brief glimpses of the far more expansive possibilities that are within our reach.

Our task, then, is to discover our unique contribution to the world and let it shine for all the world to see. And when we do it, we help others do it as well, and the light grows and grows, until it becomes a powerful force for change in our lives and in the world.

We know the secret, deep in our hearts. We've always known the secret.

> *To love one another,*
> *and all of creation,*
> *is the greatest secret of all.*
> *Love overcomes all fear,*
> *and transforms our lives and our world.*

It was in my little morning prayer — something I've done daily for many years — where I finally realized the secret in words even a child can understand. The words quietly come to me now nearly every morning. I ask for guidance, get quiet, and listen. The words are almost always the same, and they give me the greatest secret of all:

Love, serve, and remember.

Remember what? I ask.

Remember to love and serve.

When I hear the word *serve*, I'm often reminded of a great poem by Rabindranath Tagore:

I slept and dreamt that life was joy.
I woke and found that life was service.
I acted, and behold! Service was joy.

Sometimes I hear that poem in my mind; sometimes I hear other words.

Remember love overcomes fear.
Love opens the gates of heaven.

We have a choice between love and fear. Love rises above fear and opens us up to far greater possibilities, to a higher awareness and power.

Remember who you are:
a child of God,
an essential part of a miraculous creation.

47

Einstein famously said, "We can look at it as if nothing is a miracle, or as if everything is a miracle. I choose the latter."

*Remember that love finds
the perfect partnership
in all we do.*

Partnership is the key, not only to great success in the world, but to a life well lived, the most fulfilling life imaginable.

This is the greatest secret of all:

*Loving and serving yourself and others
is the key to fulfillment, happiness,
and peace.*

It has been told over and over, of course, in countless traditions throughout the world. Christ put it simply and clearly:

*A new law I give unto you:
Love one another, as I have loved you.*
— John 13:34

This new law of Christ's is one of tolerance and compassion for all, based on love for all creation, all life. When we follow this law, we find the peace within us, the peace that passes all understanding, and we find the way to create peace in our lives and in the world.

Buddha realized the greatest secret of all, and lived it and talked about it thousands of times, over fifty years of teaching:

***When you wake up,
you are filled with love and compassion.***

You might find different words. What, in your words, is the greatest secret of all?

This is a good question to ask, because it can lead you to fulfill your greatest dreams and live the most exquisite life possible.

Once you ask the question, you begin to see answers everywhere. The entire universe is a celebration of the greatest secret of all: the secret of *life*. It is love, of course. Love is the driving force of all of creation.

The answers are everywhere: In the plant

on your windowsill, your cat in the sun, a tree, the ocean, a sign by the side of the road, a phrase you hear or see somewhere, anywhere at all. This is from *Bangkok Haunts*, a mystery novel by John Burdett:

> *When you tear away the last veil*
> *you know with certainty*
> *that love is the foundation*
> *of human consciousness,*
> *that there really is nothing else.*
> *It's our constant betrayal of it*
> *that makes us crazy.*

Amen!

All worthwhile philosophies, all great religions, all great works of art lead to love.

As Leo Tolstoy wrote, "The task of the writer is to seize the readers by the back of the neck and force them to love life."

Life and *love* are synonymous. *Life, love, God, Allah, Jehovah, Creator, the All, Christ Consciousness, the Buddha Mind, the Great Mystery, the Great Goddess, Nature, Spirit, the Tao, the*

quantum field, the plenum void, Presence, Being
— all these words are interchangeable.

All great philosophies, religions, and art lead to the greatest secret of all:

> *We are created in love,*
> *by love, and for love.*
> *We are sustained in an endless*
> *ocean of love.*

Ramana Maharshi, one of the leading lights of India in the last century, put it so simply and sweetly, in one of the most beautiful phrases ever said:

> *The end of all wisdom is love,*
> *love,*
> *love.*

PART ONE

*Discovering the secret of manifestation
in your own words,
and applying it in your own way*

When we use our imagination properly
it is our greatest friend;
it goes beyond reason and
is the only light that takes us everywhere.

— SWAMI VIVEKANANDA

You will become as great
as your dominant aspiration. . . .
If you cherish a vision,
a lofty ideal in your heart,
you will realize it.

— JAMES ALLEN

THE LAW OF MANIFESTATION

There are no secrets, just truths and powerfully creative laws that remain hidden from us until we are ready to understand them. There is nothing new in these laws and truths; they have been taught for ages. The Bhagavad Gita, one of the most ancient books ever written — at least 5,000 years old — put it this way:

> *I use the word* secrets
> *not because these things are hidden*
> *but because so few people are prepared*
> *to hear them today.*

No one is keeping these laws secret. Teachers, writers, spiritual leaders, and successful people have been writing and talking about them for thousands of years. They have tried to show people the secrets in the best ways they could, and I am giving you the secrets in the clearest words I can find. But most of humanity has not been able to understand — until, possibly, *now*. What used to be considered esoteric is now solidly in the mainstream, understood and embraced by millions of people worldwide.

The secret of manifestation is not complicated — in fact, it is very simple, which is one reason why so few people understand it. It appears too simple and too obvious, and we feel it should be more complex somehow, or at least more original — not something we've heard many times before.

It can't be that simple, our thoughts whisper. *A child can understand that. It's got to be more complicated. If it's so simple, why haven't more people realized it? There's got to be more to it.*

Or it seems strangely puzzling or enigmatic when we hear it. It doesn't make sense. Or it seems to be just words, a grand-sounding idea that has nothing to do with the hard realities of our lives. And so, even though we have heard the law over and over, it remains a secret that is quickly brushed aside and forgotten. It has had no impact on our lives — until, possibly, *now*.

The simple law of attraction and manifestation has worked for a countless number of people, and it can work for you as well. The key is to put it in your own words and apply it in your own way.

How can you describe the law of manifestation in your own words? Once you can do that, you can understand the secret and put it to good use.

> *Once we can express this law*
> **in our own words,**
> *we can truly understand it*
> *in ways that have the power*
> *to affect our lives.*

I can only give you my words. If they work for you, that is wonderful. But most of you have to take my words and change them, add to them and subtract from them, using the vocabulary you're comfortable with, before you can make the secret your own.

Here is how I describe the law of manifestation, as simply and clearly as I can, in language that works for me:

> *We are powerfully creative beings.*
> *When we focus our conscious mind*
> *on a dream or goal,*
> *our limitless subconscious mind*
> *gets to work,*
> *and shows us, step by step,*
> *how to reach that goal.*

The law of manifestation is as much a law as the laws of physics — in fact, the law of manifestation incorporates the laws of physics and chemistry, and is an essential part of all the natural laws that work together to create this extraordinary planet and our phenomenal bodies, with their physical, mental, emotional, and spiritual aspects. Just the fact that we are capable of understanding these words, and of using them to become wonderfully creative, is a miracle in itself, beyond words to truly describe.

The law of manifestation is the miraculous law of creation. The exact ways this law operates to apparently create something out of nothing will remain a great mystery for years to come, but regular people with little or no education — even you and me — can easily apply this simple law in our lives.

Here's another way to describe it — again, these are the words that work for me, and you may have to change some of my phrases to find the right words that work for you:

Great success is the result
of a great many small steps,
all moving toward a clearly defined goal.
This is the secret of manifestation.

I'll repeat: I know some of you are still thinking it can't be that simple. Or you're thinking you've heard it all before, and there's nothing new in it. And it's true — there is nothing new in this, and you've probably heard it all before. And it is simple. For me, it has to be simple. Once I can express these things in words a child can understand, then even I can understand them.

I am certain this is the process: Once we can consciously understand and express this idea in simple words, our subconscious mind accepts it and begins operating with it, and our subconscious mind is limitlessly powerful. It is connected, after all, in some mysterious way, to the whole of creation. It has the power to show us how to take whatever steps we need to take to live the life of our dreams.

There are many different ways in which this secret can be told. Here is another:

We have the power within us
to clearly imagine
what we wish to attain.
The more often we focus
our powerful thoughts
on our dreams and goals,
the closer we come to realizing those dreams,

because the steps we need to take
become obvious and doable.

How can you describe the simple and profound law of manifestation in your own words?

Once you can do that, you understand the secret. Once you understand it, what are you going to do with it? What kind of life do you want to create for yourself? The choice is yours to make, and you have limitless possibilities to choose from.

THE FOUR SIMPLE STEPS TO MANIFESTATION

Over the past thirty years, I have developed a very simple system to help us manifest our dreams. It has been assembled from many different sources, as you will see. Take it in, then change and adapt it as you wish.

This system has four steps that can be summarized in four powerful words: *dream, imagine, believe, create.*

Dream

It all begins with a dream, which at first is nothing but an ephemeral idea in our minds. It all begins with simply allowing ourselves to dream, *daring* to dream.

Henry David Thoreau said it beautifully and clearly nearly two centuries ago:

> *Of course you need*
> *to build your castles in the air.*
> *That is where they should be.*
> *Then you put the foundations under them.*

That sums up this entire process. First you dream, then you take whatever steps you can toward that dream, and along the way you create a solid foundation, step by step.

What happens as soon as we dare to dream? Doubts and fears rush in, realistic or — worse yet — cynical thinking rushes in, and our dreams are quickly squelched. So we have to learn to set those doubts and fears aside, at least for the moment. We'll deal with them later. We have to learn to set aside even our realistic thoughts, and let our inner dreamer, our inner visionary, be free to imagine possibilities.

The little process I suggest — the simple exercise that worked for me initially — is to take a sheet of paper and write *Ideal Scene* at the top. Put aside your doubts and fears and even "realistic" thinking for a moment, and imagine five years have passed and — inspired by this book and by so many other things in your life — you have created the life of your dreams.

Let your imagination freely roam, without any restrictions. Let your spirit soar. Let it be *ideal*, at first. We'll deal with reality soon enough. As Stephen Covey put it in *The Seven Habits of Highly Effective People*,

Begin with the end in mind.

Look at it as a worthwhile experiment. It only takes a few minutes, and yet this little exercise has a great power in it — the power to change your life and your world.

*Take a blank sheet of paper
and write* Ideal Scene *at the top.
Imagine five years have passed
and everything has gone as well
as you could possibly imagine.
What does your life look like?*

What is your *ideal*? What kind of life do you
have, ideally? What do you do? What do you
have? What have you accomplished? What kind
of person are you? Where do you live? What
does a typical day look like?

Does your ideal scene include a life of ease? If
so, include that, and keep this thought in mind:
It is possible, I assure you, to create a wonderfully successful life and career and still have a
life of ease, with plenty of time for family,
friends, and yourself.

Begin with the dream, with the ideal, and *keep
it in mind*. A dream seems so insubstantial at
first, and yet our lives and careers are built on
dreams. Our world is built on dreams.

Imagine

We have dreamed about our castle in the air; now we need to imagine how we can build it, starting with a strong foundation in solid ground.

This step became obvious to me as soon as I read through my ideal scene. Within it were a number of goals, and I needed to list them clearly. This was the next step, and it was simple to do:

> *Take another sheet of paper,*
> *write* **Goals** *at the top,*
> *and list every goal you can think of*
> *for the next few years.*

A simple list of goals. That's all there is to it.

Maybe that's all you'll need to do: Put your dream, your ideal scene, into a list of steps you need to take to get there. List your goals, and take the next obvious steps toward those goals.

When I first listed my goals and stared at them for a while, I saw that the next obvious step for me was writing those goals as *affirmations*, as if they were already happening, in that moment.

Write your goals as affirmations.

Write them in a way that is believable to your subconscious mind. It is believable that, from this moment on, you *are now becoming* something far more expansive. You're not saying to your subconscious mind that you have arrived somewhere or attained something, because you know your subconscious mind doesn't really believe it.

I am now a millionaire is something your subconscious mind would probably have difficulty accepting if you're scrounging to pay the rent every month. Word your affirmations in ways your subconscious mind can accept, as if you're *in the process of becoming or creating* what you want in life:

I am now becoming successful, doing what I love.
I am now creating total financial success. That's
worded in a way your subconscious can accept.
That's a powerful affirmation.

We can add that wonderful secret to fulfillment
from Catherine Ponder:

> *Begin or end your affirmations with*
> **In an easy and relaxed manner,**
> **in a healthy and positive way...**

Repetition of those four words — *easy, relaxed,*
healthy, positive — in itself overcomes a great
many of the fears and doubts that arise when we
move into new territories in our lives. *It isn't*
easy, our fears whisper. *It isn't relaxed — it's*
stressful! But we can get to a point where we can
say to those fears, *Yes, it is easy and relaxed,*
healthy and positive — I have affirmed it a thou-
sand times, and it is now true in my experience.

Affirmations are powerful. Every word we say,
and every word we think, has creative power in

it. Thoughts lead to actions that can bridge the gap between our castles in the clouds and our foundations here on solid earth.

Another powerful phrase to include in your affirmations is *in its own perfect time, for the highest good of all*. Even if we have a clear, specific goal in mind — our income for this year, for example — it is still good to remind ourselves that everything is unfolding in its own perfect time and for the highest good of all.

I affirm that *my company is increasing its profits by 50 percent this year, in an easy and relaxed manner, in a healthy and positive way, in its own perfect time, for the highest good of all*. My subconscious mind seems to have no problem with the apparent contradiction of affirming a specific amount of income for the year and then adding *in its own perfect time*. It feels good to me, in fact, to add those words: it reminds me that the growth of my company involves the same natural laws as everything else that is growing and thriving, and the company will grow and thrive in its own way, in its own perfect time.

And it's good to close with what some of us call the "cosmic insurance policy":

This or something better is now manifesting in totally satisfying and harmonious ways for the highest good of all.

This or something better is now manifesting. Keep telling yourself those words, and they'll become true in your life.

Carry your list of affirmations around with you. Keep it in front of you. Repeat your affirmations often to imprint them on your subconscious mind.

Then just relax, kick back, and watch the miracles unfold. You have discovered the secret of manifestation. You have it within you, in your ever-creative imagination.

The first step is to dream; the second is to imagine how those dreams can possibly come into being. We have our list of goals — now how do we realize those goals?

The secret is to draw up a blueprint, a plan.

To build anything, you need a blueprint.
The secret is to make a plan.

How do you go about this, exactly? Maybe you can just sit down at this moment with each major goal and make a brief plan to reach that goal. But before that, there's another little exercise that might open up whole new worlds for you: Listing *What Ifs*. This great little trick is something I adapted over time from Lenedra J. Carroll's powerful book *The Architecture of All Abundance*. Like the other action steps above, it takes just a few minutes.

Sit down, take a piece of paper, and write your dream or goal at the top. Then list every *What If* you can think up — every expansive possibility that would move you toward your goal. For growing my company's profits, for example, two *What Ifs* might be *What if we publish a huge bestseller by a promising new author* and *What if we branch out into more electronic publishing and dramatically increase the content we have on the Web?*

Lenedra Carroll says to try to come up with twelve *What Ifs*. I usually come up with between three and, at the very most, eight. The exact number certainly doesn't matter. Just brainstorm for a while and list as many *What Ifs* as you can.

Watch it open up all kinds of creative possibilities, and within some of those creative possibilities you will see steps you can take that aren't that difficult — in fact, they're simple and obvious. Take those steps, and you're on your way.

For each major goal you have, explore as many possibilities as you can. Then write a simple one- or two-page plan to reach that goal.

For every major goal,
write a one- or two-page plan.

What steps do you need to take to reach your goal? Maybe at first you can see only a few things you need to do. As I mentioned in the Introduction, when I first did a plan to create a successful business, all I could think of was to read a used Business 101 textbook and talk to people who knew more about business than I did and ask them naïve questions. Once I did that, the next step became obvious: Write a simple plan, on one page of paper, of the steps I needed to take next to start and build a successful company.

Like every other exercise in this simple system, this doesn't take long and doesn't require a lot of words. The simpler, the better, in fact. Keep your plan short, so you can keep it clearly in mind and your subconscious can grasp it and accept it.

Don't worry if your plans seem incomplete at first. More will be revealed as time goes on. Don't think that what you're writing is etched in stone, because you can and probably will keep changing your plans over time.

Make a plan,
then take the next obvious steps
in front of you.

Your plan is your blueprint. When you write it, you are asking your subconscious mind how you can be successful doing what you love to do, and when you ask that question you start getting answers. Your powerful subconscious mind will show you, step by step, what you need to do to bring your ideas and dreams into reality. And they are the perfect answers for you, because they come from within you.

If someone asks you, "What is your plan?" you should be able to give a clear answer in just a minute or two. When you can do that, you convince your subconscious mind that you intend to move toward that goal, and your powerful subconscious gently and quietly guides you, showing you the steps you need to take next to reach your destination.

We dream of our castle in the air, then we make a blueprint of it, a plan to build it, on just a few sheets of paper. Within that plan, we always see the next steps we need to take to move us toward the realization of our dreams.

Believe

My wife gave me a picture frame that had the secret of manifestation stamped on it in those four powerful words: *Dream, Imagine, Believe, Create.*

When I first read those words, an inner voice said, *That's the entire process, in four words.* But then I thought, *It's really summed up in three words. There's nothing to* believe *in this process — you do it and you see that it works.*

I never had to make a leap of faith or come to believe in this process, just as I never had to take a vow to believe in the laws of physics. I took these few little steps and watched it all set into motion. I never had to believe in the power of affirmations, or writing my goals and plans, or imagining my ideal scene; I simply tried them and found that they helped make some pretty remarkable changes in my life.

The truth is, *all* the practices and techniques that we've heard about over the years work: affirmations, prayers, declarations, positive thinking, creative visualization, self-actualization, self-realization, whatever you want to call it. They all work because *every thought we have is a powerful creative force.*

The only problem is that our doubts and fears can be powerful creative forces in our lives as well, if we let them. I'm sure the process works like this: We affirm, *I am now creating success, doing what I love to do, in an easy and relaxed manner, in a healthy and positive way.* And the Universe — or our subconscious mind, or whatever you want to call it — says *Yes!* And it goes about showing us just how to manifest our dreams, revealing to us exactly the steps we need to take.

But then, if our next thought is, *Oh, but it's so hard to succeed. So few people are really doing what they love to do...,* then the Universe says, *Yes, it's true — it's very hard for you, with those thoughts. Look at how hard it is. In fact, it's getting worse all the time.*

Every thought we have, for good or ill, is creative. As soon as we focus as much or more on our dreams as we focus on our doubts and fears, our dreams — through a process that will always remain mysterious — begin to be realized, one step at a time.

We can sum it up this way:

> *Even though there is nothing to* believe
> *in this process,*
> *we have to become aware*
> *of the beliefs we have,*
> *and see how they operate in our lives.*
> *Once we identify those beliefs,*
> *we can change them into more supportive,*
> *powerful beliefs that help us realize*
> *our dreams.*

We don't have to make a leap of faith. We don't have to *believe* in this process, just as we don't have to believe in physics to see it operating in our lives.

But it is essential to become aware of the beliefs we carry with us, and see how much they affect every moment of our lives. Even just becoming aware of these beliefs is a great step toward letting them go, if we wish, or changing them into much more powerful, positive beliefs.

I used to believe I was a fool with money, totally out of control. It was certainly true in reality: In my twenties, whatever money I made immediately vanished. In my mid-thirties, the company I had founded was teetering on the edge of bankruptcy, and I had $65,000 of credit card debt and was not making enough to pay even the minimum monthly payments on the stack of cards I had.

I went through a process then that changed my life. It is called the *Core Belief Process*. Like the other things that worked for me, the process was simple; all it involved was answering a few questions honestly. When I did, I became more consciously aware of my limiting beliefs about money and success.

The final steps of the Core Belief Process led me to the affirmation that completely countered those limiting beliefs: *I am sensible and in control of my finances. I am now creating total financial success, in an easy and relaxed manner, in a healthy and positive way.*

After I affirmed that a few thousand times or so — especially when my doubts and fears were assaulting me — I saw a great shift in my life, a quantum leap. Money was no longer something mysterious beyond my control, and managing money became simple and obvious. I started to see how easy it was to be sensible and in control of my finances, and I found I was on my way to creating financial success.

That is the power of the right affirmation, repeated enough times that your subconscious mind accepts it as true. A simple affirmation can change your beliefs and change your life. Even if you don't believe it, just try the following little process and see what happens.

The Core Belief Process

This activity can help you deal with any difficult situation or problem in your life. All it requires is answering these questions as honestly as you can, either in your head or on paper:

1. *What is the problem?* Just describe the situation, for a minute or two.

2. *What emotions are you feeling?* Just name them, in a word or two. Is there fear, frustration, anger, guilt, sadness? Sometimes just the act of naming the emotions will be enough for you to let at least some of them go. At other times, you have to go through all the steps of the process before your emotions shift.

3. *What physical sensations are you feeling?* Take a minute to tune in to your body. Briefly describe what you feel happening physically.

4. *What are you thinking about?* Take a few minutes and say out loud or write down what has been going through your mind. Is there a repetitive stream of thoughts you've been having lately? What are those recurrent thoughts?

5. *What is the worst thing that could happen in this situation?* What is the worst-case scenario that you can imagine? If that happened, what would be the very worst thing that could happen to you? It is good to shed some light on your deepest fears, because you come to realize

that the chances of those deep fears actually being realized are very slim indeed.

6. *What is the best thing that could happen?* What would you like to have happen ideally? What is your ideal scene for this area of your life?

7. *What fear or limiting belief is keeping you from creating what you want?* Now we're getting to the core of the problem: What fear or limiting belief can you identify? State it as simply as you can — the simpler, the better. *I'm a fool with money. . . . I don't have what it takes. . . . It's so hard to succeed. . . . It's all so stressful and unhealthy. . . .*

8. *What affirmation can you come up with that counteracts that negative or limiting belief?* Put it in directly opposite words, if you can. Play with it until you find an affirmation that feels good to you and speaks to you in your own unique way. *I am sensible and in control of my finances. . . . I am creating total financial success. . . . I am now creating abundance in my life. . . . I am living the life of my dreams, in an*

easy and relaxed manner, in a healthy and posi-tive way.

9. *Say or write your affirmation repeatedly over the next days, weeks, and months.* Write it down and put it in places where you see it often. Re-peat it — or repeat them, if you have several — in the morning and throughout the day when-ever you remember, especially when doubts and fears arise, as they almost surely will. When you repeat it enough, it will become more pow-erful than your doubts and fears.

When I went through this simple process, startling changes started to happen almost im-mediately. I didn't have to *believe* the process worked because I saw it working in my life, in an easy and relaxed manner, in a healthy and positive way.

This secret is told simply and clearly in the Bible, in the book of Job:

> *And you shall decree a thing,*
> *and it will be given unto you.*
> *And light will shine upon your ways.*
> — *Job 22:28*

We have heard so many of these things over and over. Now these ancient truths are beginning to be realized in the lives of a large portion of humanity. Once we see the power we have to affect our own beliefs, we see that we can change our lives — and change the world as well. We see, in fact, that we have everything we need in this moment to realize our greatest dreams. We find that we have within us the ability to dream a lofty dream, affirm that it is coming true, and take the steps necessary to realize it.

We've come to the final step in the secret. This step takes the castles we have created in the air and fully builds them, on a solid foundation, in the real world.

Create

Here are the final suggestions to uncover the secret of manifestation and make it a powerful tool for growth and expansion.

Keep remembering what you know: Remember to begin with the end in mind, and keep it in mind always. Never forget your dream, and keep imagining how that dream can possibly be realized. Let your imagination soar. Keep reviewing the plan you wrote for each goal, and rewriting if necessary.

Here's a key to success to incorporate into your written plan — it's completely obvious when you think about it, but something so few people seem to know:

> *Develop a multipronged strategy*
> *for each goal,*
> *one that doesn't take no for an answer.*

First, you'll try this. If that doesn't work, you'll try that. There are endless possibilities for you, endless creative ways you can realize those dreams of yours. Try *something*. Don't be afraid to fail, because if that attempt doesn't work, you can always try something else. Keep trying, and eventually you'll find something that works.

Focus on your plan,
and be persistent.
That is the secret to success.

Here's another simple, obvious thing you can do: Look at your plan, take your weekly calendar, and make sure you have something each week in your calendar that moves your plan forward. It can be the simplest thing, and it doesn't have to take long to do it. But do something nearly every week (except when you're on a vacation) to move ahead.

When you take those first few, tentative steps, you'll notice a shift in your thinking. What before was an intangible dream, an ephemeral fantasy, is now becoming a clear goal — and then, over time, it becomes an *intention*. You've proven your intention by taking the steps you have taken. Your subconscious accepts your intention, and starts to show you exactly what you need to do next to create it in your life.

It is a mysterious process, but it is also very simple. There is no higher math involved. Your level of education doesn't matter. Your past experience doesn't matter. When you have a clear plan, in writing, your subconscious mind will show you, step by step, what you need to do to bring your ideas and dreams into reality.

You have everything you need to create the greatest success in life that you can imagine: a miraculous body, a phenomenal brain, and a vast and powerful subconscious mind. Now it is just a matter of focusing your mind in the right direction, setting your course, and correcting your course when necessary. That's worth repeating in bold, and remembering:

*You have everything you need:
a miraculous body, a phenomenal brain,
and a vast and powerful subconscious mind.
Now it's just a matter of focusing your mind
in the right direction.*

That sets our course. Then what happens? We get frustrated or anxious or overwhelmed, and we forget our course. We forget our dream, over and over. We fall back into old habits, and forget where we want to go. So we have to keep correcting our course, over and over, just like a pilot does on an airplane.

We have to remember our dream, again and again, and remember our plans — that gets us back on course. If we keep doing that, again and again, we are bound to reach our destination, sooner or later.

Why has this secret proven so elusive for so many people? All it requires is daring to dream, and daring to plan a path to realize that dream, and then taking the next obvious steps in front of us.

How many people dare to imagine their greatest dreams? And of those who do, how many actually sit down and write a plan to reach that dream? Very few. And yet the process is so simple — and it leads us, step by step, to creating the life of our dreams.

This is the secret of manifestation. The process is mysterious, because it involves the miracle of creation, but setting the process in motion in our lives is a simple matter indeed.

Go for it! Stretch out — body and mind — and reach for your highest dreams. You will never regret it, for in the process you grow so much and so quickly that, in many ways, you become a completely different person.

You become *self-actualized*, as Abraham Maslow put it. You are no longer a student; you have become a master, in your own absolutely unique and original way.

You reach your full potential as a human being and are willing and able to contribute, in your own way, to the evolution of humanity and the blossoming of our world.

PART TWO

Discovering the greatest secret of all
in your own words,
and living it in your own way

A new law I give unto you:
Love one another,
as I have loved you.

— JOHN 13:34

The end of all wisdom
is love,
love,
love.

— RAMANA MAHARSHI

THE GREATEST SECRET OF ALL

There are far more things in heaven and earth that are far more important than the law of manifestation. Countless people have discovered the secret of manifestation and still have miserable lives, filled with pain and frustration.

Look at the lives of some of the wealthiest people in the world, and you see lives full of misery, because so many of them haven't learned the simple secret of a life well lived, a life of happiness and inner peace, a life of purpose, a sacred and miraculous life.

Millions of people throughout human history have known this secret — and have known that it is the greatest secret of all, far more important than any other. And every one of them has tried to pass it on to others. The words have been written and spoken loud and clear in millions of different ways, including in every great spiritual tradition, East and West — in Christianity, Buddhism, Islam, Hinduism, and indigenous traditions around the world. And it is being told by a great number of teachers and leaders in the world today. There is nothing new in it; it is the perennial philosophy. It is simply that most people aren't prepared to hear it.

We've all heard it many times,
but we forget, over and over,
until we find it in our own words
and finally remember
to live it in our own way.

I knew it as a child, but then forgot it. I learned it as a teenager, and again as a young adult, over and over, but I forgot it, over and over. It wasn't until well into maturity that I learned the secret in a way I remembered, and continue to remember every moment.

The lasting awareness of the secret finally came to me through my morning prayer. For you, it may be different. You may have different ways of discovering it and different words to express it.

The secret may dawn on you when you simply listen to your intuition, that calm and clear voice within you. It may be revealed to you when you finally understand in a new way a phrase you've read somewhere or heard someone say many times.

Christ and Muhammad learned it through prayer; Buddha learned it through meditation. Some have learned it in nature, some in churches, temples, mosques, and synagogues; some have found it through having a child, or taking on some other great task; some have learned it in books and films, conferences and talks.

Einstein discovered it purely through science and mathematics — and a tremendous amount of imagination. Mother Teresa discovered it through a simple vow. Martin Luther King, Jr., discovered it through the words of Christ. Gandhi discovered it through the Bhagavad Gita, the "Song of the Divine."

Suzuki Roshi and Thich Nhat Hanh and so many others learned it through quiet meditation. Riane Eisler learned it through her study of anthropology. Eckhart Tolle found it in the depths of his own suicidal despair. Ramana Maharshi found it by asking himself the question, "Who am I?"

People in twelve-step programs have learned it by connecting with a *higher power*. I once heard someone in a twelve-step program say, "If you don't believe in a higher power, go and try to make a blade of grass." Or a cricket. Or a galaxy.

It doesn't matter what terms you use to describe the greatest secret of all. It can be told in a vast number of ways. They all lead to the same place, however: showing us how to look within for the answers, for the guidance and inspiration we need. We find the secret through our imagination; we understand it through our own words and experience rather than anyone else's. Every teacher of the secret can only point the way, because the answer is within us.

Each of us discovers it in our own way, in our own language. I use the words *God* and *Creator* and even *Universe* at times. I use those words to describe the power and force that has created this amazing universe. We can describe it with physics, with chemistry and mathematics, without using spiritual language. The words and symbols don't matter in the least; they just point the way. Change my words and find your own.

The secret is always revealed to me in a simple prayer. Nearly every morning, I step outside, look around, and let all thought go with a single, deep breath. Then I wander around the yard, and say a little prayer. It usually starts with, "Thank you, Creator, for this beautiful day..." and goes on to list a few things I am grateful for.

"Thank you for that hummingbird zipping by. Thank you for those blades of grass, so green and vibrant, and that new flower...." And I become aware that my gratitude list could go on forever. I could spend the rest of my life naming things to be grateful for, and I would hardly have begun.

So I move on, and let the thoughts of gratitude go. I have some more silent time, so that the prayer arises from silence. Then I say the simple words that lead to the greatest secret of all: I quietly whisper, *Guide me, Creator. Guide me.*

And I listen for any quiet words that come to mind. They are almost always exactly the same, and I have come to see, over the years, how the greatest secret of all is expressed in these simple words:

Love, serve, and remember.

Remember what? I ask.

Remember to love and serve, always.

I can remember where I've heard those words before. *Love, Serve and Remember* was the title of a book by Ram Dass years ago.

Remember that love overcomes fear.
Love opens the gates of heaven.
The Kingdom of Heaven is within.

Love overcomes fear — I recognize this from *A Course in Miracles.* And I remember again that we have the choice, every moment, between love and fear. We can choose, consciously, to love. It is the far better choice, always.

Remember who you are:
A child of God,
an essential part of a miraculous creation.

I remember how much I love my children, how much I want them to be happy, fulfilled, and free. And I realize that God has the same love for us that we have for our children. We are the result of a great act of love, conceived in love, sustained by love, and if we so choose, filled with love, every moment.

I remember science's phenomenal discoveries: We are all part of a vast, single quantum field; we are in reality one with all that is. We are able, in ways that will ever remain mysterious, to affect this field and change our realities, literally create another world.

We are an essential part of a miraculous creation, eternally connected to that creation. We are a part of God, and have powerfully creative abilities because we are connected to the source of all creation.

> *Remember:*
> *Love finds the perfect partnership*
> *in all we do.*

Riane Eisler gave us this part of the puzzle in her brilliant books *The Chalice and the Blade* and *The Power of Partnership*. She gives us what she calls a *lens* through which to view the world. Do we see partnership, based on love and respect, or do we see some kind of domination or exploitation, based on fear and on a need to control?

Partnership is the solution to our personal and even global problems. For our personal problems — our anxieties, doubts, and fears — we can find that partnership with *ourselves*, with our intuition, our spirit, or whatever you want to call it, that supports us and loves us as much as we love our own children.

For our global problems — hunger, poverty, and war — the solutions are only to be found in new and better ways of working in partnership in every relationship we have: with our intimate partners and families; with our work, our community, our nation, and our world; and with nature and Spirit as well. Through partnership — and only through partnership — we can create a world that works for all of us.

The great work ahead of us, Riane Eisler reminds us, is replacing the well-entrenched model of domination, based on fear and a need to control, with a new way of living, a new model of partnership, based on love and respect for all people, and for all of creation.

I am filled with gratitude for Riane Eisler's work, and the great discovery it is based on:

Living and working in partnership
is the key to solving our global problems.
Ultimately, partnership is
far more powerful and effective
than domination and exploitation.

Living and working in partnership means loving and serving ourselves and others, and that is the key not only to a life well lived but to global peace and prosperity as well.

This is the course, after all, that Jesus took, and Buddha, and Gandhi, and Martin Luther King. Love and serve your neighbors. Love and serve even your *enemies*. Why does that still seem to be such a radical idea? Perhaps someday — I pray it is within my lifetime — this country will have a president who actually follows the words of Christ. All our presidents have called themselves Christians, but not one of them has truly followed the words of Christ.

How can you possibly invade another country and still call yourself a Christian? Christ would never build an army, attack and kill others, for any reason. He was very clear on this: *"Peter, put away your sword. If you live by the sword, by the sword you die."* Our leaders have forgotten the teachings of Christ, and they keep sending their children into war.

If we had a president who actually followed Christ, he or she would say to the world, "How can we love and serve each other? That's the only way we can solve the problems we have. We have been good partners, in many ways, with many people. But we have also been dominators and exploiters in many ways, with far too many people. How do we move beyond that, into partnerships that work for all of us?"

This is the key to global peace and prosperity, which is what we all really want, in the long run:

The key to global peace and prosperity is to replace acts of domination and exploitation with acts of partnership.

Partnership, after all, is always more powerful than domination in the long run. Our acts of exploitation and other attempts to control other people result only in endless conflicts and obstacles and problems, because they inevitably lead to frustration, anger, hostility, and resentment. The result is an endless chain of violence and suffering.

Working in partnership leads to countless creative ways to interact with each other; it leads inevitably to harmony, mutual support, prosperity, and, yes — always — *love and respect*.

Love is the creative force in the world, after all. When we work in partnership, things go smoothly, beautifully. The more we work in partnership, the closer we come to a world that works for all of us, where we all have the essentials of life — including *life, liberty, and the pursuit of happiness* — and are supported in reaching our dreams. That is a world that works, and we can create it only through partnership, and not through any form of domination or exploitation.

As R. Buckminster Fuller pointed out, we now have the capability to feed and house and support everyone on the planet. We have the technologies available for *every one of us in the world* to move up to what the great psychologist Abraham Maslow called *self-actualization*.

Maslow realized that humanity can be seen as forming a great pyramid. Over the years I have adapted his ideas somewhat — here's my version of Maslow's pyramid: The people on the bottom need food, shelter, and medical care. Those needs dominate their consciousness, and it is very difficult to move up the pyramid without having those needs fulfilled. The people a little higher need security. Without it, it is very challenging to move up and create more satisfying lives. Once those basic needs are met, we move up the pyramid into the realms of education.

We certainly have the capability to have good, free public education for all. We certainly have the money, as soon as we realize that investing in education is far more important than burning through money in warfare and other types of domination and exploitation. The two best things a country can do for its national security are to work in partnership with other countries and to have great education and vocational support for its own people.

We have the technology. We have everything we need to create an excellent educational system, from cradle to grave, for education is an endless process, finally leading us to the top of the pyramid, to *self-actualization*.

This is where we're finally able to focus on fulfilling our dreams, passion, and purpose. Whether our dreams are artistic, entrepreneurial, humanitarian, or spiritual, when we've reached this level — when we've had enough education to see the expansive possibilities that are before us — we find the encouragement and support we need to fulfill our potential. We have reached the top of the pyramid, and are able to contribute to the world, each in our own unique and creative ways.

We can create a world that works,
through partnership with all,

*by moving beyond all forms
of domination and exploitation
into creative partnerships with everyone,
locally and globally.*

My mind is filled with all kinds of creative ideas in my morning prayers, including how to have a world of peace and prosperity.

Sometimes I ask, *What is my purpose in it all?* I've reflected on this for years, and asked many other people to reflect on the question as well, for it is another way to discover the greatest secret of all.

What is your purpose in life? Many people have trouble with that word, *purpose*; it seems so serious, so *heavy*. You can substitute the word *mission* if you wish. Or *vocation*, which comes from the Latin word for *calling*, What is your calling? This is a great question to ask.

When I ask that question, I'm given a great key to a life well lived:

*We have a great purpose in life —
a great mission, vocation, and calling.*

We are here to reach our full potential,
to evolve as much as possible,
and to contribute to the betterment
of humanity.

We are here to move upward in the pyramid of consciousness that Maslow described, until we become self-actualized, self-realized, and able to help many others move up to realize their potential, and help make this world a better place for all.

Our purpose is to grow as much as we can, for on the way we are discovering new possibilities for humanity. Our purpose is to contribute in some vital way to the well-being of all. As so many have discovered, when we love and serve others in some way, our own sense of well-being, and our resources, and our joy of life expand vastly.

As Charles Caleb Colton wrote nearly two hundred years ago:

*If universal charity prevailed,
earth would be a heaven, and hell a fable.*

Our purpose is nothing less than personal and global evolution. This is all very serious stuff, and so sometimes Spirit lightens things up, and I hear Bobby McFerrin singing Meher Baba's famous quote:

Don't worry, be happy.

What wonderful guidance! How simple can it get? Or I hear it put in this way:

Remember the joy of Being.

This always reminds me of the words of Eckhart Tolle, in *The Power of Now*, a book that guides me every day and will continue to be my guide for the rest of my life: "*The happiness that is derived from some secondary source is never very deep. It is only a pale reflection of the joy of Being, the vibrant peace you find within as you enter a state of nonresistance.*"

I often think that all I need to do is to truly, deeply understand and remember these two powerful sentences from *The Power of Now* and I will know how to fully live — and even how to die — in peace and with grace.

Sometimes in my mind I hear the words of Ramana Maharshi, one of the greatest teachers in the history of India and the world. Whenever I hear those words, I have the feeling that they are the most beautiful words ever said, in any language:

> *The end of all wisdom*
> *is love, love, love.*

That is the greatest secret of all. Sometimes I hear it whispered quietly in my mind in these words:

> *Loving and serving*
> *yourself and others is the key*
> *to happiness, fulfillment, and inner peace.*
> *This is the greatest secret of all.*

This is the key that overcomes our fears and leads us to a life of grace and ease, a miraculous life.

It is a miracle, isn't it? A collection of trillions of atoms and molecules working in amazing partnership with each other wrote these words in a time now long past, and at this moment your amazing collection of trillions of atoms and molecules is sitting with these ink marks on paper and absorbing them into your mind, creating new synapses in your brain that literally change the way you think, act, and experience life. All life is a miracle, far beyond our ability to understand.

But we can learn to understand its secrets, and to work with them to create better lives for ourselves and a far better world for all creatures, great and small.

You know the secret now. Say it to yourself, in your own words. And remember it, always. It will guide you, every moment, to fulfillment, whatever that may mean for you.

It will guide you to the top of the pyramid of humanity, to a place of peace and power.

It will show you how to create the life of your dreams and contribute in your own wonderful way to making the world a far better place.

The secret is love. Love is the creative force of all life, and love is all that matters. Everything else fades into insignificance and passes away; love and life alone are eternal.

That is the greatest secret of all, the secret to a life well lived — a precious life, a sacred life, where we realize the miracle of *what is*.

It is love, always and forever.

SUMMARY

The greatest secret of all

There are no secrets, just truths and powerful laws of creation that remain hidden from our awareness until we are ready to hear them.

The law of manifestation is just as concrete as the laws of physics — in fact, the law of manifestation incorporates the laws of physics and chemistry.

We have the power within us
to clearly imagine
what we wish to achieve.
The more often we focus
our powerful thoughts
on our dreams and goals,
the closer we come to realizing those dreams.

The law is not complicated; in fact it is very simple. This is one reason why so few people understand it: It appears simple and obvious, or strangely enigmatic and puzzling. And we've heard it a thousand times before.

I am telling you the secret in the best way I can. To put it to work in your life, you need to put it in your own words. How do you understand and describe the simple and profound law of manifestation?

Here's one way I describe it:

We are powerful creative beings.
When we focus
our conscious mind on a goal,
our limitless subconscious mind
gets to work and shows us the way,
step by step, to attain our goal.

Find your own words to describe the secret of manifestation, and watch it work in your life.

Of course there are far greater secrets than the law of manifestation: the secrets of a life well lived, the secrets of happiness and inner peace, the secrets of a life of ease and fulfillment, a miraculous life, a sacred life.

Here is the greatest secret of all, in my words — take it in, and then express it in your own words.

We have a great purpose in life —
a great mission, vocation, and calling.
We are here to grow, to evolve,
to reach our full potential
and contribute to the betterment
of the world.

This is what has remained a secret for most of humanity: We are far greater than we think we are. Our potential is vast. Most of us have just barely begun to realize who we are and what we are capable of. We have had just brief glimpses of the far more expansive possibilities that are within our reach.

Our task, then, is to discover our unique contribution to the world and let it shine for all the world to see. And when we do it, we help others do it as well, and the light grows and grows, until it becomes a powerful force for change in our lives and in the world.

There are three very simple things we can do to realize the greatest secret of all in our lives:

Love, serve, and remember.

Remember what?

Remember to love and serve, always.

Remember: Love overcomes fear. Love rises above fear, and opens us up to a higher awareness. Love opens the gates of heaven.

We have heard it so many times, but we forget it, over and over:

The Kingdom of Heaven is within.

Remember who you are:
A child of God,

an essential part of a miraculous creation.
Remember that love finds
the perfect partnership
in all we do.

To love is to respect and cherish all of creation, and to rise above fear and the need to control, to rise above all forms of domination and exploitation into endlessly creative partnerships with all. We choose the cup of life instead of the sword of fear — in the words of Riane Eisler, we choose the chalice, not the blade.

Remember the brilliantly shining words of Ramana Maharshi:

The end of all wisdom is love, love, love.

This is not just some great moral advice, something to do because we want to be good; this is the very practical, down-to-earth key that opens the doors to a new life and a new world, and shows us the great view from the top of the pyramid of humanity.

*In everything you do,
love and serve yourself and others.*

This is the secret that guides you every moment to create the life of your dreams and a world that works for all. This is the end of every path of study, every worthwhile philosophy.

This is the greatest secret of all:

*Loving and serving
yourself and others
is the key to fulfillment,
happiness, and inner peace.*

You know the secret now. Put it in your own words, and remember it, act on it, and live it.

Together, working in partnership, we can discover how to live the life of our dreams, and along the way help create a world of peace and prosperity for us all. This is worth repeating and remembering:

*Together, working in partnership,
we can discover how to live
the life of our dreams,
and along the way help create
a world of peace and prosperity for all.*

ABOUT THE AUTHOR

On the day he turned thirty, Marc Allen cofounded New World Library with Shakti Gawain. He has written numerous books, including *Visionary Business*, *A Visionary Life*, *The Millionaire Course*, and *The Type-Z Guide to Success*. He has also recorded several albums of music, including *Awakening*, *Breathe*, and *Solo Flight*.

He is a popular speaker and seminar leader based in the San Francisco Bay Area. For more about Marc, including his free monthly tele-seminars, see www.MarcAllen.com.

For more about his music (including free samples), see www.WatercourseMedia.com.

For more about New World Library, see www.NewWorldLibrary.com.